Fires Were Started....

Amelia Jensen Payseno

Presentation by *BookLeaf Publishing*

Web: www.bookleafpub.com

E-mail: info@bookleafpub.com

ISBN: 9789357212410

First edition 2023

*I dedicate this book to my kids Lily and Tom
and to my love Adam.*

*Tom, keep jumping off bridges, writing books,
and being weird.*

*Lily, keep your stubbornness and sweetness and
always fight for what you want.*

*Adam, let's chase squirrels down some rabbit
holes. I love you forever. My lobster.*

ACKNOWLEDGEMENT

I acknowledge my space on Planet Earth and claim it.

PREFACE

Challenge everything you know to be true. Listen to the trees branches sway in the wind. Fall in love with yourself. Don't hold anything back. It's time.

Spiderweb

hanging between two trees
underneath the twilight moon
a new piece of art arrives in
Autumn's museum.
meticulously the architect
hangs her masterpiece
Peering through
gossamer windows
woven of silken lace,
she waits silently.
will it capture some
unsuspecting prey
in its web of lies?
sucking out its soul,
leaving a black hole,
emptiness.
or will the parabola
collapse on itself,
demolishing
the masterpiece
She so scrupulously created
leaving her tired and
needing to start over?

Atoms

I didn't take you seriously, thought you were joking. That day we walked home in the soaking rain as if nothing could change. If I had known it was the last time I would ever touch your face, I'd remember what you said, but the words are scattered all over the place. I thought I found a home in you, a warm fireplace to come home to. You always said we were insignificant, specks of atoms in a universe as magnificent as this, the sky in the background looks like its mourning and the little stars adorn it, your ashes blow across the earth into the vast continent that gives birth to the cold winter days.

Gypsy Girl

I once knew a gypsy girl who curled up next to
lonely old me by the fire.
The rare warmth of a woman who spoke the
same language as me, silence.
She slipped in like a shadow by the moonlight,
where everything is more youthful, romantic,
mysterious. I never gave her a key to my room
but she carried the key to my heart on a gold
necklace.My tiny gypsy girl needing so little to
be happy, never changed her soup-stained
clothes. When we flew the kite with the tail of
doves she was the happiest I've ever seen,
thought she would fly away.
Sometimes the wind whispers her name, but I
lose it every time though it's at the tip of my
tongue, I swear.They took her away from me,
murdered by the Nazis in Treblinka, my gypsy
girl. I made it my life's work to destroy their
literature, the way her absence destroyed me.
Deciding on a poetic death I suddenly
remembered her name, Ilona. It bloomed in my
thoughts like a gypsy rose.

End of the Drought

walk this parched desert
with me
Tell me all that you see
some days the sun is too bright
don't know what to do with the light
I walk this planet alone
looking for a place to call home
I'm not denying that I will die trying
to find out where I belong
I'm the puddle after the rain
The rivers you trace in my veins
The lotto ticket that ran out of luck
The cigarette after a good ****
The painting in a crappy motel
The spring from an artesian well
What if I find my way
and you don't wanna stay
The stars go out one by one
The threads are coming undone
Sometimes it's such a chore
to understand what all this is for
Time's running out
I'm full of doubt
You're the drug that I'm craving
If I am worth saving
is this the end of the drought?

Ode to Daylight Savings Time

anxiety defined:
humans myth
of the meaning of time.
a maximum security prison
created in our minds
raspy voices yelling
do more, acquire more, prove that you're worthy
of existence
playing on repeat we feel the defeat
creating clocks
to plan, to control,
to package life's unplanned circumstances into
minutes, hours, days
contraptions syncing our heartbeat to the
tick-tocking of the second hand
translating into doubt because time's running out
trapped in timeline documenting every
heartache, every slap in the face, every fall from
grace
living in a state of hunger for the past,
ruminating about the future
narcissistic, codependent
a toxic relationship
red flags littering the landscape

until you hit rock bottom you may not ever
know
moments that change your life can't be captured
in a butterfly net or planned on a calendar
the way a stream meanders through the valley
the way a breeze brushes your cheek
the vastness of the expanse
of how the breath and soul and join with nature's
heartbeat
you realize
there is no time,
only serendipity
moments come at you when you least expect,
knock you to the ground screaming unconscious
or wrap you in a cozy blanket by the fire,
handing you a cup of tea
or do nothing at all
when you break the chains of time and sense the
flow of the universe within, your heart and soul
open to love, spontaneity and flow
and you embrace the connected consciousness
within every human and living thing
without expectations
and that is..
timeless

Heartbreak

The heart takes the journey and the mind
follows. As for the one who is left behind, it's
going to hurt, bruise purple and black. Like any
fresh wound it heals as the little hand on the
clock ticks through the mourning of a deceased
hope. Scars become permanently tattooed onto
the soul. The door to friendship can no longer be
pried open. Love and pain live in the same place.

Packing my Belongings and Longings

Out of the hundreds I ran across, few have touched me that way, sensually, intellectually. I sit on the bare cold ground replaying the same love song because like being left, it's what I know. I'm an expert at it. I'm packing my bags and moving my belongings and longings. The only place we can meet now is on the periphery between sleep and consciousness, in black and white dreams.

Sometimes slivers of memories appear but I don't know what they mean. I can hear you calling my name but I can't find you. A question mark devoid of closure. When I startle awake I feel you in the ache of my bones, persisting no matter how many pills I gulp down. And yet, I have no regrets.

Dark Night of the Soul

Today seems especially heavy
Sadness feels like a crescent moon
dangling at the end of a peice of string in my
chest, carrying the weight of the things I tasted
but can never have again
The shape of her ballerina silhouette
The way she danced through life effortlessly,
luscious lips, the vintage edition of a bittersweet
cabarnet
blue-green eyes churning with desire for life and
all it's pleasures and sorrows
months of tear stains on the corners of the pillow
All left behind in room 8
I can see a faintly lit bulb swing back and forth
as I walk towards her room
In the old Communist hospital
Paint peeling, water stains, tiles barely in place
The sheets have been replaced,
A new patient moans in her bed, eats from her
tray
I feel a raging hatred towards him, I want to rip
out the tubes
and tell him to disappear

But they can't get the scent out of the last words
she vomited, they can't get the scent out of her
watered-down perfume
It lingers like her ghost
Telling me to get on with life
"There's nothing left for me to give when I'm
dying"
The moon's edges are sharp, poking at me, blood
dripping
I accept it as is and go about my day
Despite the pain
I manage to work, eat, draw
Angela asks me if I understand the meaning of
my lunar emotion, the metaphor in my body
"Maybe", she says, "it's the faint light of hope
hanging on by a thread"
Maybe, I think, this what Jung called the dark
night of the soul?

Fire Alarm

I'm wiping the bathroom mirror clear of
yesterday's disappointments,
leaving behind a pristine surface to start fresh,
anew.
Having to face my reflection I am caught
unaware, realizing something inside has
changed. I don't recognize myself anymore.
Yearning to hold onto memories, I reach out to
touch something real but it's gone.
I can usually sense people's energies but I don't
sense yours, it's like you're far away or fading, a
lost signal, as if someone blew out the lit match,
but it wasn't me. I swear it wasn't me. I only let
the smoke waft until it sounded the fire alarm.

Ode to Prosser, WA

As the sun melts into the pink-orange sky,
silence falls on the desert. The snake slithers into
its hideaway. I roam these parched hills by dawn
as the chinook wind caresses my face. The wild
horses used to roam here. The tribes that used to
fish here by the river, christened it Tap-Tut.
Offering assistance as guides who follow the
moon, never found the boy who got lost
wandering though they searched for days. I
make my way to the other edge of this dwelling,
transformed into a ghost town by night, keeper
of stories passed. The abandoned buildings with
boarded-up windows, invite critters to make
their home here, littered with skeletons and
secrets. The old mill, once providing
nourishment for the town, now collapses under
its own weight. The railroad tracks that haven't
seen a train in decades beckon, "come close".
Come hear the long gone promises of gold dust
down by the river, where men either died or
struck it rich, only to lose it all later. And there is
Roza, the mysterious yet ever present stranger
who's name is etched into the old railway
station, several buildings and even a street, yet
all we know is she was a famous companion, a

daughter of a railway baron. The ghost lady
wanders gravity hill. Raped and murdered in the
mill, she led a bus to its demise, the marks of the
rubber tires still etched in the concrete. The
graves of children scatter the landscape, having
been moved from their original resting place
when the bomb was created.Tanks still leak
chemicals, they flow towards the river soon to
fill it with poison.The coyotes howl, the snakes
slither, the chinook wind whispers The town
slowly awakens. Like a cactus in full bloom

Ode to Adam

Part 1

Extraordinary love story written ages ago, manifesting during an eclipse and coming into fruition at the airport. So near yet so far apart for decades. Souls deeply intertwined and feeling like home in each other's arms. Bliss.

Part 2

A visual depiction of our complex minds, thousands of light bulb moments combined, connected by a string of facts you can't unwind. Circuits trip when our fingertips touch. 24 hours, 220 watts. Acorns of knowledge like squirrels we chase. Even though that line seems out of place, our energy brightens any space.

Part 3

With you, I'll learn how to feel at home here on Earth in a warm log cabin with a cozy fire and allow myself to breathe the fresh mountain air. With you, my mind and body will reconnect and my soul won't waft away like steam from a cup of coffee. With you, my thoughts won't race like squirrels running across a keyboard, 11 tabs open on the screen. With you, I'll join in on

small talk, laugh at the sub-text and enjoy it.
With you, I'll feel comfortable in my own skin
without going blank and staring off into space
when I'm triggered. Your hand reaches for mine.
I'm grabbing it and never letting go. I will let
you love me.

Part 4
This is it,
the point in our lives
where love eclipses fear
this morning I heard you whisper in my ear
My soul's taking flight, like Amelia Earhart,
I feel weightless in space and time
Our souls intertwine
Love rushes in with the tide
We'll conquer the world side by side

Bars Around My Soul

There was a time in my life when I walked the streets alone, fists up, armor around my heart. I fought back whenever anyone provoked me, feeling justified and brave. I found friends with ragged clothes and dirt on their faces. We banded together like a pack of hyenas, feeling wronged by the world. The moment I thought it turned was the moment I ran, sprinting as fast as I could through vast spaces and hiding in a place I thought was safe. But it only lasted for a little while. I was dragged back like a prisoner with no hope of escaping. Bars around my soul, bars keeping me from seeing what was really outside, a world where normal people lived in normal houses with white picket fences surrounded by something I couldn't name, affection. Living in a fantasy world in my mind, I escaped into castles with moats on a deserted island. But I'm not resigned to my destiny, I don't always have to be an orphan of the night. I can stand at the precipice at the edge and jump in. I can swim to the other side instead of drowning. It's my choice, not yours. It never has been yours.

Jurek Szczurek

Pewien maly Jurek Szczurek
znalazl w piwniicy ogorek
i pyta tate Jurka Szczurka
czy mu wolno zjesc ogorka
tata szczurek odpowiada
"ogorek szczurek nie jada"
od ogorek brzuszek boli
i szczurkowi nie pozwolil

White Rose

Every 3 months
in a cyclical ritual at dusk
Shrouded in the mist of mystery
a white rose surfaces
On the ice cold headstone
where her name is etched in bronze
Like clockwork
the love story is
rewritten in secret ink
dripping down the page
I wonder how many tears
erased the trace of passion
nobody knows who
yet everyone understands
why
The white rose sleeps
And fades with the seasons
only to reappear later
wind scatters the petals
Like a blanket covering her body in
unrequited love
The answer we seek
lies within the white rose
On an ice cold headstone
holding tight to the secret

within its petals
in silence

Derailed

When life derails me
and takes me off track
I catch the train to yesterday
the rhythm is soothing
to my anxious mind
The rolling scenery mixes
with precipitation on the windows
rolling raindrops obscure my vision
allowing me to fill in the remaining
landscape of what was and could have been
I stay silent and disappear among the passengers
looking for a story to enter into
but nothing is written with me in mind
I depart in the dark
not caring which town I end up in
I drift with the wind
as it blows my hair around
the rain soaks me to my core
the train whistles and leaves with
all of my burdens and sorrows
on car number 84

Poland and WWII Trauma

The summer air here is moist and heavy. You can feel it every time you walk on the cobblestone paths. Death still lingers in the air, fresh wounds, permeating the way people interact, unknowingly passing down attitudes, feelings and behaviors to the subsequent generation. (These inherited fears, the nightmares that keep us awake sit in the parenthesis in the paragraph of our lives). We can't run or hide no matter how hard we try. They seep into the political landscape, creating warring factions since someone has to take the blame. Foreign onlookers and children absorb disdain and hurtful words like a slap in the face. Repression oozes and denies truth creating laws to hide atrocities. Striving to be better than, creating an us and them mentality, they shut out people who have every right to belong, forming narratives to ease their inferiority complex. A third of the nation, skeletons of who they could be if they could feel. Souls full of holes they fill with alcohol, the illusion of busyness and the quest for wealth. Fragmented selves drifting in the wind like Autumn leaves, the light of their soul, extinguished. They sit in the abyss waiting to be reconnected. Will they accept or recognize help even if it comes? The nation needs the world to say I'm listening, you've been hurt, you matter. But will it ever happen?

Wagrowiec

a tydzien bede we Wagrowcu.
Dni sie gonia. Walizka juz spakowana.
Spotkamy sie przy skrzyzowaniu rzek? A moze
przy slynnej piramidzie? A moze jednak
znajdziesz mnie w malym rynky na
Kasprowicza, szukajac jakiegos skarbu? a
tydzien Cie spotkam poza ekranem, jesli granice
nie zamkna przez Delte. A ja, z maska na
twarzy, lece linia lotnica o tym samym imieniu
wleczac sie autobusem, a potem wiecne godziny
wsrod chmur. Czasai smierc ma skrzydla i silnik,
jak serce, sie lamie. A czasami wiatr za
skrzydlami pcha nas w nowe przygody.

Winter Love

Snow falls gently on a quiet December morning
It sparkles like glitter when the sun peeks out
The geese trumpet their announcement, it's time
to fly South
You and I in the midst of it all,
hide in our snow globe enclave
protected from the world,
We create our own safe haven
Laying in each others arms, soft carresses and
cocoa kisses
Mezmorized by each other's eyes, taking in our
breath down to our toes, thawing what was
frozen
Our snow globe is filled with music of 2 lovers
creating a song
You can shake up our world but we are
oblivious, even as shards of glass fall to the floor
Even as the Snow Queen casts her spell.
Creating Eden with you is my only dream,
weathering storms, hanging Christmas
stockings,
You as the Grinch, me as Cindy Lou Hoo and
our Noble hound
Safe in your arms
I finally know it's going to be ok

www.ingramcontent.com/pod-product-compliance
Lightning Source LLC
Chambersburg PA
CBHW070726160726
48003CB00006BA/2393